Mimi Dietrich

BALTIMORE BLOCKS
for Beginners
A Step-by-Step Guide

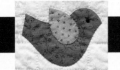

Dedication: To all of my students for your enthusiasm and inspiration!

Baltimore Blocks for Beginners: A Step-by-Step-Guide
© 2012 by Mimi Dietrich

Martingale®
19021 120th Ave. NE, Ste. 102
Bothell, WA 98011-9511 USA
ShopMartingale.com

Printed in China
17 16 15 14 13 12   8 7 6 5 4 3 2 1

**Library of Congress Cataloging-in-Publication Data
is available upon request.**

ISBN: 978-1-60468-172-7

Mission Statement

Dedicated to providing quality products and service to inspire creativity.

CREDITS

President & CEO: Tom Wierzbicki
Editor in Chief: Mary V. Green
Design Director: Paula Schlosser
Managing Editor: Karen Costello Soltys
Technical Editor: Ellen Pahl
Copy Editor: Melissa Bryan
Production Manager: Regina Girard
Illustrators: Ann Marra & Laurel Strand
Cover & Text Designer: Adrienne Smitke
Photographer: Brent Kane

ACKNOWLEDGMENTS

This book is based on a class I teach in Baltimore, where I live. Through this class I help students get started on a fun appliqué journey, and in turn, numerous students and friends have contributed to my own journey by inspiring the colors and quilts in this book.

Many, many thanks to:

- Bob Dietrich for his wonderful quilter-husband patience!
- Libbie Rollman for volunteering to make a quilt with a very tight summer deadline.
- Emily Pelton for making her first Baltimore block with me.
- Norma Campbell for hand quilting two quilts.
- Maria O'Haver for machine quilting four quilts.
- Karen Brown for machine quilting two quilts.
- Robbyn Robinson, Patty Stenpeck, and Alice Isenbart for fabric and design ideas.
- Judy Sullivan, Mary Anderson, and Janice Reece, students whose Baltimore blocks inspired some of the projects. (I just loved their fabric choices!)
- Everyone at Martingale who believes in me and makes dreams come true!

CONTENTS

Introduction

Welcome to Baltimore-style appliqué! This guidebook will help you take your first steps on a wonderful journey. Within these pages, you will discover techniques for creating a successful quilt design with hand appliqué. I hope you enjoy the process as you learn to stitch perfect shapes. And I hope these first steps will give you confidence and encourage you to try other techniques and designs.

I've lived my entire life in Baltimore, Maryland. Thirty years ago I saw an exhibit of antique album quilts at the Baltimore Museum of Art and I was instantly inspired. I could not believe the wonderful colors, small appliqué stitches, and beautiful quilting designs—all created by women in my hometown nearly 150 years before. I immediately fell in love with appliqué! That exhibit greatly influenced my life as a quilter.

The original Baltimore Album quilts were made in the 1840s and '50s. These quilts are called *albums* because each block in the quilt is a different design—like the variety of photos in a picture album. Many of the blocks were appliquéd with floral wreaths, baskets, and vases. The blocks were often made by several quilters working together to make a large quilt. They used many colors, but predominantly red and green. Many of the quilts have survived in excellent condition, perhaps because they were used only for special occasions.

I've taught Baltimore Album appliqué classes in the Baltimore area and around the country for three decades now. My first students made quilts using a pattern with four small blocks adapted from the antique quilts. Since 1990, I've taught a yearlong class in which students create full-sized quilts using a variety of traditional, contemporary, and dimensional appliqué techniques. Lately, to prepare students for the yearlong class, I've been teaching My First Baltimore Block, taking them slowly through the techniques and elements of a basic appliqué block. Now, with this book, you can take my class—anywhere and any time!

I am always thrilled to see a student finish a block. I know the time it takes to appliqué the designs as well as the many decisions to make about fabrics, colors, techniques, settings, and quilting designs. Completing a block is always an accomplishment, and it is particularly special when a student finishes an appliquéd quilt block for the very first time.

This book contains my favorite appliqué techniques. I believe they are wonderful methods for successful beginnings. You will soon discover that there are many techniques, tools, and patterns for appliqué. All of these techniques are correct, as long as you are comfortable and pleased with the results. Your challenge will be to try them and decide which ones you like the best. I always tell my students, "It's your quilt!" You can reproduce the colors and techniques in an antique quilt, or you can use your favorite contemporary fabrics and methods. Appliqué is fun, creative, and a great way to express yourself!

I enjoy making appliquéd quilts, but my true passion is to be involved with students making these quilts in Baltimore. I love to inspire quilters, to help them choose colors, learn appliqué techniques, gain confidence, get excited about the process, and, in a sense, repeat history. I have had the very special opportunity of connecting quilters here in Baltimore with quilts that were made in our city long ago.

This book provides a basic Rose Wreath pattern that will help you learn how to appliqué stems, leaves, berries, buds, flowers, and a bird as you make a small quilt. I have also included two extra patterns plus a gallery of quilts that use the same basic elements and techniques. There are suggestions for variations on the basic pattern and some dimensional techniques, giving you permission to express your creativity by changing some of the pieces in a design.

If you're a teacher, I hope this book becomes your teaching tool to start quilters on a journey through appliqué. If you are a student, go at a careful pace and stitch one element at a time as you work your way through a small quilt. Invite your friends, gather them together, and take your first steps into a place in Baltimore's quilting history with me!

~Mimi

My First Baltimore Block, appliquéd and hand quilted by Mimi Dietrich

My First Baltimore Block

This section contains the basic materials list and cutting instructions for making your first Baltimore block and sewing it into a quilt. Before you begin, be sure to read through "Fabrics for Your First Baltimore Block," beginning on page 11, as well as the specific instructions that follow. The text will walk you through the process, from choosing and cutting fabrics to adding borders and a label, just as if you were taking my class.

FINISHED QUILT: 28¾" x 28¾" • FINISHED BLOCK: 13" x 13"

MATERIALS

All yardages are based on 42"-wide fabric.

1 yard of multicolored inspiration print for setting triangles, outer border, and binding

Several fat quarters* or ¼-yard pieces of assorted prints for appliqué pieces: stems, leaves, flowers, buds, berries, and bird

1 fat quarter* or ½ yard of fabric for appliqué background

¼ yard* of accent fabric for inner border

1 yard of fabric for backing

33" x 33" piece of lightweight batting

Scissors, needles, thread, thimble, and freezer paper**

A fat quarter is a piece of fabric approximately 18" x 20". A ¼ yard of fabric is 9" x 40".

**See "Appliqué Supplies" on page 14 for additional details.*

CUTTING

Be sure to read "Cutting Guidelines" below before cutting your fabrics.

From the multicolored inspiration print, cut:

2 squares, 10¼" x 10¼"; cut in half diagonally to yield 4 half-square triangles

2 strips, 4" x 21¾"

2 strips, 4" x 28¾"

3 binding strips, 2¼" x 42"

From the appliqué-background fabric, cut:

1 square, 15" x 15"

From the inner-border fabric, cut:

2 strips, 1¾" x 19¼"

2 strips, 1¾" x 21¾"

From the assorted prints for appliqué, cut:

Stems, leaves, flowers, buds, berries, and bird

From the backing fabric, cut:

1 square, 33" x 33"

CUTTING GUIDELINES

Wash and press your fabrics before cutting to ensure that they will not bleed and that your cutting will be accurate. Please read "Fabric Preparation" on page 13 for additional details.

Cutting the Background

The final, finished background for your Baltimore block will be 13½" x 13½" square to include ¼"-wide seam allowances on all sides. However, because appliqué blocks sometimes fray or distort during stitching, I like to cut the squares about 1" larger to start and trim them to the correct size after the appliqué is completed. For your first Baltimore block, you will cut the square 15" x 15".

To easily cut a 15" background-fabric square with a regular 6" x 24" ruler, follow these steps.

1. Cut your fabric with scissors or a rotary cutter so that it is roughly an 18" square.

2. Fold the square into quarters.

3. Place the two folded edges on vertical and horizontal lines on your cutting mat. Measure 7½" over from one folded edge, align your ruler with the lines on your mat, and carefully cut the edge that is not folded.

4. Reposition your ruler and repeat to measure 7½" over from the other folded edge. Cut the remaining edge that is not folded. When you unfold your fabric, you will have a 15" square!

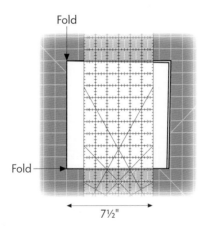

Later you will trim your block to 13½" square before adding the setting triangles and borders.

Cutting the Appliqués

Turning to page 16, follow the instructions in "Getting Ready: Making the Full-Sized Pattern and Templates" and "Cutting and Preparing for Appliqué" on page 19 to cut the various appliqué pieces.

Cutting the Borders

The cutting list provides exact measurements for cutting all border pieces. You may want to cut the borders an inch or two longer and then trim them to the exact size of your quilt center later. You can also wait to cut the borders until after the quilt center is complete.

Fabrics for Your First Baltimore Block

The best place to shop for appliqué fabrics is your favorite quilt shop. Take this book with you, and you'll find quilters who will be happy to help you choose the right fabrics.

Many traditional appliqué quilts are predominantly red and green on a cream background, but this is your quilt—you can make it in any color combination you like! Make sure you look at the photos in the quilt gallery beginning on page 46. The variety of color choices will inspire you.

Select fabrics made of 100% cotton. They are easier to appliqué than synthetic fabrics, which fray more than cotton and are often slippery. Printed fabrics are great for appliqué projects—the printed designs help to hide your stitches. You may love solid colors, but for your first Baltimore block I suggest using prints, or tone-on-tone prints that look like solids.

When you are looking at potential fabrics for your appliqué quilt, you will need to think about four categories: an "inspiration fabric," the background fabric, the appliqué fabrics, and the backing fabric.

INSPIRATION FABRIC

The inspiration fabric is the fabric that you fall in love with when you go shopping! It's the fabric that makes your heart sing. It has all your favorite colors. It's a beautiful floral, a multicolored geometric design, a perfect border for your project—a printed fabric that will help you select a variety of additional fabrics for your color scheme. The inspiration fabric will make up the setting triangles, outer border, and binding of your quilt; in essence, it determines the color palette for your project.

Inspiration fabrics often have colored dots along the selvage. These dots were used during the printing process, but you can use the dots as an aid in choosing matching fabrics for the appliqué pieces. Look for fabrics that go with the colored dots and your project will look very coordinated. If there are no colored dots, simply match appliqué fabrics to the colors you love in the inspiration fabric.

Colored dots along the selvages are helpful when choosing coordinating fabrics.

Sometimes inspiration fabrics are part of a designer collection from a particular fabric company. Ask if your quilt shop carries the coordinates; they will be perfect for your project.

BACKGROUND FABRICS

Background fabrics for appliqué are usually light, solid colors or small-scale prints that coordinate with the appliqué design. Avoid choosing prints or stripes that are too bold; they may compete with the appliqué design.

Choose a background fabric that complements your inspiration fabric and color palette. White background fabrics add brightness and clarity to pastel appliqués. Off-white backgrounds enhance the richness of darker appliqué palettes. Subtle prints are lovely choices for stitchers who prefer a textured, rather than solid, appearance in the background. A fabulous tea-dyed print can give quilts an antique glow. Appliquéing onto a dark background creates a dramatic effect.

If you choose a white-on-white background fabric, select one with a somewhat open pattern. Sometimes you can feel the design "painted" on the surface of the fabric. You might have trouble hand stitching through the white print if the design is too dense.

Traditional cotton quilting fabrics are wonderful for appliqué. If you love batiks, be aware that they have a tighter weave, sometimes making it a challenge to push the needle through the fabric. For batiks, I suggest a thinner needle (size 11) and thread (size 60) for your project. For your first Baltimore block, it will be easier to use a traditional cotton background. If you want to use batiks, reserve them for appliqués only, rather than for the background.

APPLIQUÉ FABRICS

Traditionally, Baltimore-style appliqué blocks are made with a palette of red and green fabrics, plus touches of blue, pink, brown, and golden yellow. This color scheme is always appropriate, but it's also fun to create the designs in soft pastels, brighter folk-art colors, or varied shades of a single color or two, such as blue or even black and white. Your inspiration fabric determines the color palette, so always look for appliqué fabrics that coordinate with that print.

Solid-colored fabrics might seem safe to use, but printed fabrics make designs exciting. They also help conceal stitches along appliqué edges and add dimension to your appliqués. Fabric printed in multiple values of one color can be very effective when used for flowers and leaves. These tone-on-tone fabrics, such as dark green printed over a lighter green, look like a solid but have subtle texture. In addition, you might find a printed design that could represent veins in leaves or shadows in flower petals.

Tone-on-tone prints add dimension to appliqués.

You'll need fabrics for each element of the Baltimore block design listed below. I've included some suggestions to help you when shopping for these fabrics or raiding your own fabric stash.

Stems: Choose a medium shade of green or brown, or a different color that coordinates with your fabric palette. A printed fabric always looks good. Stripes and plaids also look great when cut on the bias.

Leaves: Most of your leaves will probably be green. You can use one perfect green fabric for all the leaves, or as many as eight different green fabrics. You may also want to choose four greens ranging from light to dark, and place one of each leaf symmetrically on each side of the design.

Refer to the colors in your inspiration fabric to find the perfect color of green for your project. For a fall look, you can also use gold, orange, or even red and purple. For a fantasy look, try a bright blue or a black-and-white print.

Buds: The bud has two parts: the calyx (the base of the bud) and the folded portion. Usually, the calyx is green with a folded bud that matches the colors of the flower in the design. You can also make the calyx a dark color and the folded bud a lighter color to match the flower. The folded bud looks best in a solid or tone-on-tone fabric to ensure visibility of the folds.

Berries: For the berries, choose fabrics that coordinate with your inspiration fabric or the flower colors in your design. If you have a printed fabric, you may want to showcase a small motif in the center of each berry.

Layered rose: You need three fabrics for the layered rose. The largest piece is the base of the rose. This is the main color and will dictate the overall appearance of your rose. For example, if you use pink for this piece, it will look like a pink rose.

The two small teardrop petals should accent the main rose color, and have some contrast so that they show up well on the base. Pink works well on red, and, likewise, red works well on pink.

The third color, for the center of the rose, can be darker than the base color or lighter. Students often use gold or yellow for the center.

Bird: Choose light and dark shades of the same color for your bird. Sometimes you can find one fabric with areas of light and dark. For fun, choose fabrics to simulate the texture of the bird's feathers. Blue birds are always nice, but you might want to coordinate your bird with the colors in your inspiration fabric.

Other fabrics: Fabrics printed with floral images are wonderful to use because you can cut whole flowers or individual petals and leaves from them to add realism to your appliqués. Refer to "Fabulous Fabrics" on page 45. Nature prints often include flowers and leaves—and butterflies, as in "Wild Thing!" on page 52.

BACKING FABRIC

You'll need fabric for the back of your quilt. Use a plain fabric, or choose a print that coordinates with your design. A printed fabric will not only look great, but also help to hide your quilting stitches on the back. The inspiration fabric always works well as a backing. Make sure that the quality of your backing fabric is comparable to that used on the front of your quilt.

FABRIC PREPARATION

Prewash all fabric to preshrink it and to test for color-fastness. You don't want a dark red or green to run and bleed onto a light background fabric.

Wash dark and light colors separately. Sometimes it may be necessary to wash and rinse dark fabrics several times to get rid of excess dye. Many quilters use Retayne (for commercially dyed fabrics), Synthrapol (for hand dyes), or dye magnets such as the ones made by Woolite to prevent the colors from bleeding onto each other when the quilt is laundered. To test a fabric for colorfastness, cut a small piece, wet it, and place it on a scrap of background fabric. If color shows up on the background scrap, wash the fabric again, or choose a different fabric.

Before cutting, press fabrics to remove wrinkles. Cutting from perfectly smooth fabric makes it more likely that your pieces will be sized accurately. Some quilters use spray starch or spray sizing to give the fabrics a little extra body.

Appliqué Supplies

In addition to fabric, you'll need some basic equipment and supplies. The list that follows includes some of the many products available in quilt and fabric shops that will help you successfully complete your appliqué projects.

Circle templates: You can make your own circle templates out of sturdy material such as a manila folder or template plastic. You can also purchase ready-made plastic templates called "Perfect Circles." Another handy option is to purchase a plastic stencil found in most office- and art-supply stores; this stencil includes several sizes of circles, and enables you to draw perfectly round shapes on your fabric or paper.

Embellishments: Keep some embroidery floss and beads on hand for the eye of the bird and the centers of gathered blossoms and flowers.

Fabric markers: Choose from a variety of fabric markers to trace appliqué pieces and to transfer appliqué designs onto the background fabric. Use silver marking pencils, water-erasable pens, or fine-lead mechanical pencils for light fabrics. For dark fabrics, use sharp chalk pencils in white or yellow. Always test the markers on a scrap of fabric to make sure the marks can be removed easily.

Freezer paper: Freezer paper is available at most grocery stores and quilt shops. The shiny, plastic-coated side of the paper becomes soft and sticks to fabric when you apply a dry, warm iron to the uncoated side. Use freezer paper to make templates for appliqué shapes.

Glue stick: A water-soluble glue stick is handy for glue basting seam allowances as well as holding appliqué pieces in place on the background fabric.

Iron: Use a steam iron to press your fabric before you appliqué and to press finished blocks. Use a dry iron to attach freezer-paper templates to your fabric.

Needle threader: If a needle is difficult to thread, use a needle threader to insert the thread through the eye of the needle. Many quilters love the Desk Needle Threader made by Clover. It threads your needle with the push of a button.

Needles: When choosing a needle for hand appliqué, size is very important. A sharp, fine needle glides easily through the edge of appliqué pieces, creating small, invisible stitches. In needle sizes, the higher the number, the finer the needle. Use sizes 10 to 12 for best results.

Some appliqué stitchers use short quilting needles, called Betweens, because they feel that short needles offer greater control. Official appliqué needles are longer and are called Sharps; they are thin and glide easily through fabric. A longer needle, called a Straw needle or Milliner's needle, works well for needle turning the appliqué edge as you stitch it to the background. Many appliqué stitchers love this needle and feel that the longer length provides more control to neatly turn under the seam allowance. Try different needles to find the one most comfortable for you. My favorite is a #10 Straw needle.

Between ———————
Sharp ————————
Milliner's ———————————

Permanent marker: Use a fine-tipped permanent marker to trace appliqué patterns onto template plastic.

Pins: Small ½" or ¾" straight pins are wonderful for pin basting appliqué pieces to the background fabric. Because they're shorter than regular pins, they're less likely to catch the thread as you stitch.

Plastic ziplock bags: What did we do before ziplock bags were invented? They are indispensable for keeping your appliqué pieces organized and clean.

Rotary-cutting equipment: A rotary cutter, mat, and ruler will help you cut your blocks, borders, setting triangles, and binding.

Scissors: Small scissors with sharp blades that cut all the way to the point are often a stitcher's prized possession. You'll also need "paper" scissors to cut paper or plastic templates.

Sewing light: A true-color light, such as an OttLite lamp, or a magnifying light will help you see your appliqué more easily as you stitch. If you're right-handed, the light should shine over your left shoulder; if you're left-handed, it should shine over your right shoulder.

Sewing machine: Make sure your sewing machine is in good working order with a new needle when you sew your quilt together. I love a ¼" presser foot that helps to keep the seam allowances accurate.

Tape: Use Scotch Removable Magic Tape to anchor your fabric to your pattern while you trace the design onto your background fabric. Unlike other tapes, this type won't rip the paper pattern or fray your fabric.

Template plastic: Use template plastic to make patterns for multiple appliqué pieces and to make a square to trim your finished block.

Thimble: Use a thimble, if desired, to protect your finger as you push the needle through your fabric during hand appliqué.

Thread: Thread color is very important. Appliqué thread should match the color of the appliqué fabric rather than the background fabric. If you match the thread color to your appliqué fabric, it will blend in and your stitches will seem smaller and almost invisible. If you can't find the perfect color match, use thread that is a little darker. It will blend into the appliqué fabric, whereas a lighter shade of thread may sparkle and show along the edge.

Appliqué designs with numerous different-colored pieces require multiple shades of thread. For appliqué fabrics that are printed with many colors, choose a thread that blends with the predominant color. Sometimes a neutral brown or gray blends perfectly.

I believe that the best thread for stitching appliqués is 100% cotton. It is pliable and blends invisibly into the edges of the appliqués. Size 50 (or 50-weight) is all-purpose sewing thread and can be found in most stores that sell sewing supplies. Size 60 is a finer thread, which helps make your stitches invisible. If you can't find cotton thread in just the right color, use cotton-covered polyester thread. Some hand stitchers love to use thin silk thread. Experiment and see which thread you like best.

Always use white or light-colored thread for basting. Dye from dark thread can leave small dots of color on light fabrics when the thread is removed.

Tweezers: A small pair of tweezers will help you easily remove freezer paper after you've appliquéd a piece to the background.

Your favorite chair and lamp: When you hand appliqué, you'll be more comfortable and have the patience to make smaller stitches if you sit in your favorite chair with a lamp aimed at your work. A cup of tea or coffee also helps!

Making an Appliqué Pillow

One of my favorite appliqué tools is a small pillow that I place in my lap when I stitch. It makes it easy to see my work, rests my hands and shoulders, improves posture, and is a great pincushion. Here's how to make a simple pillow using a sheet of 8½" x 11" paper as a pattern.

1. Using the paper pattern, cut out one rectangle from white fabric and one from printed fabric, adding a ¼" seam allowance to all sides.
2. Sew the rectangles right sides together, using a ¼" seam allowance and leaving a 3" opening on one long side for turning the pillow. Add purchased cording (or cording that you've made yourself) around the pillow edge, if desired, to make the pillow sturdier.
3. Turn the pillow right side out and stuff firmly with polyester stuffing.
4. Stitch the opening closed by hand, and enjoy using your pillow!

Getting Ready: Making the Full-Sized Pattern and Templates

Before you take your first appliqué stitch, you need to make a full-sized pattern of the Baltimore block, mark the appliqué placement lines on your background square, and make templates for the required appliqué pieces. Working carefully and accurately will ensure that your Baltimore block is a success and that your quilt looks fabulous!

MAKING A FULL-SIZED PAPER PATTERN

The pattern for your first Baltimore block is given in quarters on pages 57–60. Follow these instructions to make a full-sized pattern.

1. Cut a 13½" x 13½" square of freezer paper and fold it into quarters.
2. Open up the square and place the center folds of your paper over the center marks on the pattern page for the first quarter. Trace the pattern onto one quarter of the freezer paper using a mechanical pencil or sharp pencil.
3. Position the next quarter of the paper on the second quarter of the pattern and trace.
4. Repeat for the remaining two quarters. You will now have a full-sized pattern!

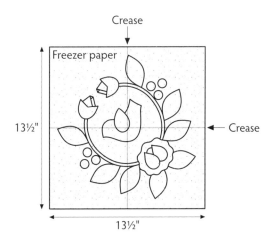

Crease

Freezer paper

13½"

← Crease

13½"

You can also photocopy each of the four parts of the pattern. Cut the pattern along the centerlines and tape the four pieces together.

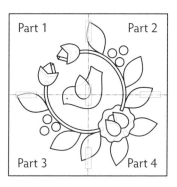

Part 1   Part 2

Part 3   Part 4

For the other block designs, "Round Wreath" and "Crossed Leaves" on pages 61–62, follow the same procedure to trace or photocopy the pattern four times and create the complete, full-sized design.

Give Your Book a Twirl

Working with appliqué patterns within a book can sometimes be difficult. The patterns may be printed close to the binding, making them hard to trace. Many of my students like to take their favorite books to a copy shop and have the regular binding replaced with a spiral binding. This makes it easy to open the book flat and trace the patterns.

MARKING APPLIQUÉ PLACEMENT LINES

To accurately position the appliqué pieces on the background fabric, you will need to trace and mark the design directly onto the fabric.

Tracing Your Design onto a Light Background

1. Using removable tape, fasten your paper pattern to a flat surface.

2. Fold your square of background fabric into quarters. Press the folds at the edges, but gently finger-press to mark the center of the block. Place the background fabric right side up over the appliqué pattern. (If you're using a solid background fabric, you can use either side.)

3. Place the folds of your fabric over the centerlines marked on the pattern, centering the design in the middle of your fabric. Tape your fabric over the pattern using removable tape.

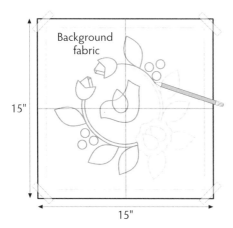

4. Trace the design exactly on the lines with a washable pencil or fabric marker. If you aren't certain that the traced lines will wash out, trace slightly inside the pattern lines. The lines will be covered by the appliquéd pieces after they are stitched, so you don't have to worry about removing the lines. Trace the design using solid or dotted lines.

Tracing Your Design onto a Dark Background

A light box is very helpful when tracing a design onto dark fabric. If you don't have a light box, tape the pattern to a window or glass door on a sunny day.

1. Center your fabric over the pattern and tape the fabric to the glass.

2. Trace the design with a white or yellow chalk pencil.

MAKING TEMPLATES

You will need a freezer-paper template for each appliqué piece, except stems and circles. Freezer-paper templates are used to shape your fabric appliqués. When

Light-Box Alternative

You can create your own light box by opening the leaves of your dining-room table and placing a storm window or sheet of Plexiglas over the opening. Position a lamp or flashlight on the floor below the opening. Place your pattern on the glass and your fabric on top of the pattern. The light will shine through like a light box, allowing you to easily trace your design.

the same motif is repeated several times, such as the leaves and buds, make a plastic template of the shape first. This helps ensure that all pieces of one shape are the same size. I also make a plastic template for asymmetrical designs, such as the bird.

To create the freezer-paper appliqué templates, you will trace each shape in the design directly from the pattern or trace around the plastic template onto freezer paper. Prepare your templates with care and accuracy to achieve the best results.

Making and Using Plastic Templates

Templates made from template plastic are durable and useful for many appliqué techniques. You will need just one template for each shape, and you can reuse the templates many times in other projects and with other methods. For your first Baltimore block, make plastic templates for the leaves, calyx (the base of the folded bud), and bird.

1. Place template plastic over the pattern and trace the desired shape on the design lines using a fine-tipped permanent marker. Don't add seam allowances.

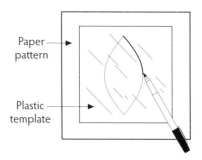

2. Cut out the plastic template precisely on the traced lines so that it is the exact size of the original piece.

3. Label the front of each template with the pattern name and template number or other identification. This indicates the right side of the template.

4. To make the freezer-paper templates, trace around the plastic template onto freezer paper with a fine-lead mechanical pencil. Trace the shape the required number of times and cut out on the lines

   Note: Because I press the freezer paper to the wrong side of the appliqué fabrics, asymmetrical shapes must be traced and cut in reverse. The bird is the only shape that is asymmetrical in this design; the instructions on page 35 are written for creating a left-facing bird as in the pattern design.

5. Store your plastic templates in a small ziplock bag.

Quick Cutting

Here's a suggestion for cutting multiple freezer-paper templates of the same shape. First, cut up to four layers of freezer paper roughly the same size as your pattern piece. Trace the design onto the top layer (or trace around your plastic template) and then staple the layers together by placing a few staples in the space that will be cut away. The staples will hold the layers together as you cut, ensuring accurate templates.

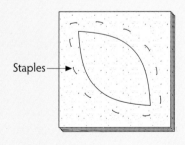

Making Freezer-Paper Templates

For one-of-a-kind pieces, like the layered rose, you can simply trace the original pattern onto freezer paper.

1. Place the freezer paper, coated side down, over the pattern, and trace each design onto the paper side with a fine-lead mechanical pencil.

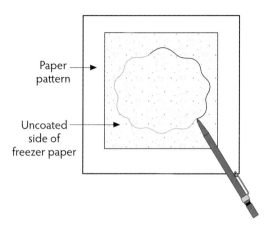

2. Cut out the templates on the traced lines so that they are the exact size of the original pattern pieces.

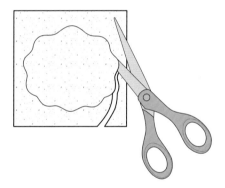

Cutting and Preparing for Appliqué

There are many techniques for preparing the raw edges of appliqué fabric pieces before sewing them to the background fabric. All the methods can be successful if done correctly, but here I will share my favorite method—using the freezer-paper templates on the back of my fabric. The freezer paper sticks to the fabric and controls the appliqué shape. I love to use this method, especially when I want accuracy in repeated designs.

PLACING TEMPLATES ON THE FABRIC

You will create beautiful appliqués if you carefully consider where to cut your fabric. The following information will help you choose the perfect section of your fabric for each appliqué shape. I have included more tips with the directions for each shape.

Straight of grain: Patterns for appliqué designs don't usually provide grain lines to aid in positioning the templates on the fabric. You can place the templates on the appliqué fabric so that the straight of grain runs in the same direction as the background fabric.

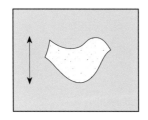

Bias: Designs that have inside points (such as hearts and the calyx of the bud) or curves (such as leaves) should be placed on the bias of the fabric. This diagonal placement prevents fraying at inside points and helps ease fabric around curves. Stems and vines are also cut on the bias to allow easy shaping into curves.

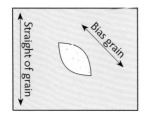

Fussy cutting: For some designs, you can cut an appliqué piece to include a specific part of a printed fabric. Quilters love to fussy cut leaves or flowers that have been printed on the fabric. In this case, disregard grain lines to enjoy the way that the fabric and the appliqué design can work together. Use a window template, described next, to help you determine where to cut.

Window template: To get a special effect from a fabric and make fussy cutting easier, trace the appliqué template onto paper. Cut out the shape and discard it, creating a window template. Move the window over your fabric to determine the perfect placement for your template before you cut out the appliqué piece.

CUTTING THE APPLIQUÉS

1. Place the freezer-paper template with the coated side against the wrong side of the appliqué fabric. Rely on the straight of grain, the bias, or a window template to help you position the template on the fabric. If you have more than one template to cut from the same fabric, leave at least ½" between pieces. Press the freezer paper onto the wrong side of the fabric using a hot, dry iron. Let the piece cool.

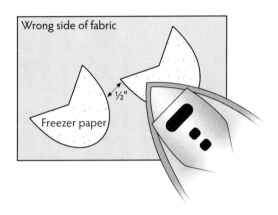

2. Cut out the fabric pieces, adding a generous ¼"-wide seam allowance of fabric around the outside edge of each shape.

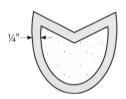

Reverse Reminder

Remember that the bird in this design is asymmetrical and must be traced in reverse in order to match the block shown. Press the reversed freezer-paper template to the wrong side of your appliqué fabric.

3. Turn the ¼" seam allowance toward the freezer paper and use a running stitch to baste the seam allowance by hand to the freezer paper. Stitch through both the fabric and the paper. You can also use a glue stick to lightly glue the seam allowance to the paper. Fold any outside points and clip any inside points to within a few threads of the freezer paper. Do not clip outside curves.

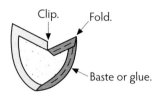

Note: If you use a glue stick for basting, you will need to wait until all appliqués are complete before removing the paper. You will also need to cut a slit in the background fabric to remove the freezer paper; you won't have the option of removing it as you are stitching.

PLACING APPLIQUÉS ON THE BACKGROUND

Now that your appliqué shapes are cut and the seam allowances are basted, you're ready to position the shapes on the background fabric and hold them in place with pins. This will keep them from shifting or moving while you appliqué. Small ½" to ¾" straight pins—sometimes called appliqué pins—are wonderful because they are less likely to catch your appliqué thread as you stitch. If you do have trouble with threads tangling around the pins as you sew, pin the appliqués in place from the wrong side of the background fabric.

I like to pin and appliqué one piece in place before adding the next piece, instead of pinning all the pieces in position and then proceeding with the appliqué. If I work with too many pieces at once, the appliqué thread gets caught on the other pieces as I stitch.

Use several pins to attach the prepared appliqué piece to the background so that it won't slip out of place. Follow the placement guide that you've traced onto your background, making sure the lines are covered if necessary.

Hand-Appliqué Stitch Techniques

After you've cut out your appliqué pieces, prepared the seam allowances, and basted the pieces to the background fabric, it's time to appliqué! This section will walk you through the detailed steps of the hand-appliqué stitch. Before you stitch your appliqués to the background fabric, however, be sure to read the important information about needles and thread on pages 14-15. Also note that for this design, the stems are the first shapes to be stitched. You'll need to refer to "Stems" on page 25 to cut and prepare the stem pieces.

THREADING THE NEEDLE

Thread is smoother in one direction than the other because it is twisted during the manufacturing process. You can take advantage of this by cutting and knotting your thread so that it will slide smoothly through the fabric. If you're right-handed, thread the needle before you cut the thread off the spool. Then measure an 18" length and cut the thread near the spool. Tie a knot in the end that you cut.

If you're left-handed, tie a knot in the end of the thread while it is still on the spool. Then, measure off an 18" length. Cut the thread near the spool and thread the cut end into the needle. No more twisted threads while you stitch!

TYING A QUILTER'S KNOT

A quilter's knot is secure and once you know how to make one, it's quick and easy, resulting in the perfect knot each time.

1. Hold the needle in your sewing hand and the end of the thread in your other hand.
2. Cross the end of the thread in front of the needle, and hold the thread end securely between your forefinger and thumb along with the needle.

Hold thread between thumb and forefinger.

3. Move the thread away from you, wrapping the thread around the needle three times.

Wrap thread around needle three times.

4. Hold the wrapped thread between your forefinger and thumb and gently pull the needle through the wraps.

Pull needle through wraps.

5. A neat knot will appear at the end of your thread.

Thread and Needle Notes

- Cut a single strand of thread about 18" long. If your thread is too long, it will tangle and you'll have unwanted knots.

- If you have trouble threading the needle, trim the end of the thread at an angle with sharp scissors.

- Try putting the needle onto the thread instead of the thread through the needle. Surprise!

Move the needle toward the thread.

- Many quilters use a needle threader—a Desk Needle Threader (by Clover) is one of my favorite tools.

- Cut a new segment of thread for each appliqué piece. It's tempting to use every inch of your thread, but it frays and loses strength with repeated stitching.

TRADITIONAL APPLIQUÉ STITCH

The traditional appliqué stitch works well on straight areas as well as on sharp points and curves, making it appropriate for sewing all areas of your appliqué designs.

1. Thread your needle as directed above with a single strand of thread approximately 18" long. Tie a knot in the long end.

2. Slip your needle into the seam allowance from the wrong side of the appliqué piece (but not through the background fabric), bringing it out through the fold line. The knot will be hidden inside the seam allowance and your work will look very tidy.

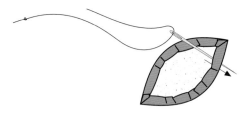

3. Start the first stitch by bringing your needle straight out of the appliqué and inserting it into the background fabric directly opposite the point where the thread exited the appliqué. You will stitch along the outer edge of the appliqué. If you're right-handed, stitch from right to left. If you're left-handed, stitch from left to right. The most important thing to think about here is to make the smallest stitches possible on the front of your appliqué.

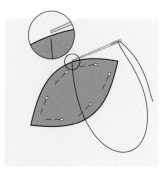

4. Move the needle forward about ⅛" under the background fabric, parallel to the edge of the appliqué. Then bring it through to the right side of the background fabric, just at the edge of the appliqué. As you continue, pierce the edge of the appliqué

piece, catching only one or two threads of the folded edge.

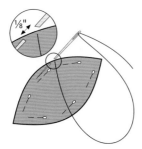

5. Insert the needle into the background fabric just off the appliqué edge. Let your needle travel forward another ⅛" under the background, bringing it up again to barely catch the edge of the appliqué.

6. Give the thread a slight tug and continue stitching. The only visible parts of the stitch are small dots of thread along the appliqué edge. The part of the stitching that travels forward will be seen as ⅛"-long stitches on the wrong side of the background fabric.

Wrong side of fabric

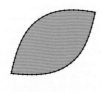

7. When you get to the end of your appliqué stitching, or you're nearly out of thread, pull your needle through to the wrong side. Behind the appliqué piece, take two small stitches, making a simple knot by bringing your needle through the stitch loops.

8. Before you cut your thread, take a moment to make the back of your work as neat as the front. Take one more small stitch behind the appliqué to direct the tail of the thread under the appliqué fabric. Clip the thread end right next to the fabric so that it won't show.

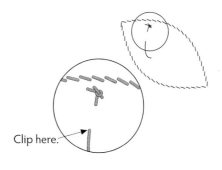

Clip here.

Stitching Tips

- Support your fabric by holding the forefinger or middle finger of your non-sewing hand directly under the appliqué. As you stitch, push the needle underneath until it gently touches your finger. Then, move the needle back up through the fabric.

- As you sew, keep your needle parallel to the appliqué edge with each forward stitch.

- Give the thread a slight tug with each stitch so that it blends into the appliqué.

- Keep the length of your stitches consistent as you stitch along the straight edges. Make stitches closer together when you get to curves and points.

- Use your non-sewing thumb to help guide the fabric onto your needle.

- And finally—stop stitching while you still have enough thread to tie a knot!

REMOVING BASTING AND PAPER

I like to remove the basting stitches and freezer-paper templates as I go. However, if you use a glue stick, wait until the appliqué is complete.

1. Clip and remove any basting stitches.

2. Cut a small slit in the background fabric behind the appliqué and remove the freezer paper with tweezers.

Note: If you do not want to cut the background behind the appliqué to remove the freezer paper, stop stitching about an inch from the starting point. Remove the basting stitches and pull out the paper from the front. Finger-press the edge of the opened space and finish appliquéing.

If you've basted with a glue stick, soak the piece in warm water for a few minutes to soften the glue and release the paper. Cut a slit in the background fabric and gently pull out the paper. After the appliqué dries, press it from the wrong side. (See "Washing Your Block" on page 37 for more on this process.)

Stitching Your First Baltimore Block

Take it slowly and work piece by piece to appliqué your first block. Appliqué pieces are often numbered to indicate the stitching sequence, but you will soon learn that the pieces follow a natural order: stems first, and then leaves, buds, and berries, followed by flowers and, finally, accent shapes such as birds.

My First Baltimore Block. Stems are appliquéd first, followed by leaves, buds, berries, flowers, and the bird.

STEMS

Stems are often the first shape to be appliquéd in a design. Leaves, flowers, and berries all follow and are often layered or placed on top of the stem. As with all aspects of appliqué, there are a number of ways to cut and prepare stems. Curved stems must be cut on the bias. Straight stems can be cut on the straight of grain, but they will fray less if cut on the bias. Stems do not usually require freezer-paper templates.

Cutting and Preparing Stems

For the Baltimore blocks in this book, you will cut stems on the bias with a ruler and rotary cutter. The stems will finish a little wider than ¼", and they will be slightly longer than you need so that you can trim them to fit the pattern.

1. Cut two bias strips, ⅝" wide x 10" long. To do this, measure 8" from both sides of a corner, and mark a dot at each position. Connect these dots with your ruler and make a diagonal cut. Move the ruler ⅝" and cut a bias strip. Repeat to cut a second ⅝"-wide bias strip.

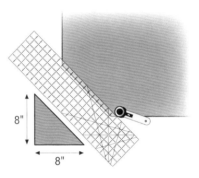

Stem Making 101

For other projects, you may want wider or narrower stems. Here's the rule: Cut fabric strips that measure twice the width of your desired finished stem. For example, for a ¼"-wide finished stem, cut the strips ½" wide.

You may want to try using a bias-tape maker if you work on other appliqué projects in the future. With this device, you can quickly make bias strips for stems and vines without basting. Spray your strips with spray starch and feed them into the wide end of a bias-tape maker. Press the folded stems as they emerge from the narrow end of the tool.

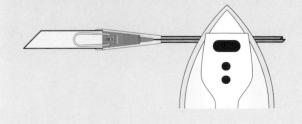

2. Using a fabric marker, draw a line in the center of the strip, on the wrong side of the fabric. This will help you turn under the correct amount of seam allowance.

3. Thread a needle with a light-colored thread that you can see clearly against the stem fabric. This makes it easy to baste and a breeze to remove the basting stitches later. Do not make a knot in your thread when basting stems. This also simplifies removal of the basting thread later.

4. Roll your fabric over your needle so that the raw edge touches the centerline, and stitch near the folded edge, leaving a tail about 2" long at the beginning. Use a running stitch and try to keep your stitches short.

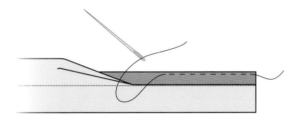

5. When you get to the end of the strip, leave a 2" tail of thread.

6. Fold the raw edges of the second side in to meet at the center, wrong sides together, and repeat the process to baste the second side. Do not press the stem strip; it will be easier to curve the edges smoothly when appliquéing if they have not been pressed.

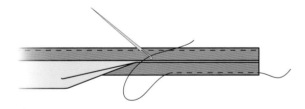

Wrap It Up for Later

If you are not ready to use the stems right away, wind them around a cardboard tube to keep them smooth and maintain the turned-under edges. This works especially well when preparing longer stems or vines.

Placing and Stitching Stems

Use the placement lines on your background square to position your stems. To hold them in place while stitching, I use a glue stick rather than pins. There is an appliqué rule stating that you should sew the inside of the curved stem first, and then the outside curve. However, a strip that has been glued down will not move or stretch, giving you permission to break the rule.

1. To easily make a smooth, curved stem with a basted bias strip, pull gently on one of the basting threads until about an inch emerges from the end of the fabric. Repeat with the basting thread at the other edge of the strip. Ease the fabric along the pulled threads to create the inner edge of the curved stem. Place the curved stem on top of the curved line on your background fabric to shape it perfectly. I love this technique!

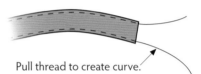

Pull thread to create curve.

2. Apply glue from your glue stick along the stem lines on the background fabric, not on the stem itself.

3. Position the stem on the marked stem line of your design, wrong side against the background fabric. The stem should extend at least ¼" into the area for the flower, bud, or berry at the end of the stem. You will sew the other appliqué over the end of the stem for a clean finish. For the first minute or so, you can lift the stem and reposition it if you need to make an adjustment. When you like the way it looks, finger-press the stem in place.

4. Referring to "Hand-Appliqué Stitch Techniques" on page 21 for detailed instructions, slip your needle into the end of the stem and bring it out at the edge of the fold. This will hide the knot and tail of thread under the appliqué. Start sewing along the straight edge of the stem.

Concealing Dark Stem Ends

🐦 If you have flowers or leaves of a very light color, dark stems could show through the light fabrics. To remedy that situation, start and end your stitching exactly on the lines, leaving the ¼" seam allowance free and unattached. Later you can go back and trim it so that it is hidden under the seam allowance of the adjoining piece.

5. Appliqué along the folded edge, using stitches about ⅛" long and keeping them as even as possible. Make sure your stitches are going through the background fabric so that the stem is attached. Appliqué both folded edges of the stem.

6. When you get to the end, bring your needle through to the back of your project, tie two small knots (see page 23), hide the thread tail under the stem, and clip the thread.

7. Remove the basting threads.

Quick Release

🐦 If your basting threads stick to the glue a bit, dab a little warm water on the stem and the threads will be released in a jiffy.

LEAVES

Leaves are the second shapes to be appliquéd to your Baltimore block. The points will butt up against the stem or be placed underneath the flower at the bottom.

Cutting and Preparing Leaves

If you cut the leaves on the bias, the curved edges of the leaves will be easy to baste and appliqué. The bias edge will ease along the curves and create a smooth shape, and the point will fold sharply.

1. Imagine a line through the center of your leaf. Orient this line on the diagonal as you place the freezer paper on the wrong side of your leaf fabric. Iron the freezer paper to the wrong side of your fabric.

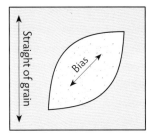

2. Cut out the leaf, adding a generous ¼" seam allowance around the freezer paper.

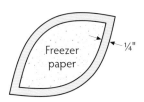

3. Hold the leaf with the fabric toward you and the freezer paper away from you. Start at one of the points and gently fold the fabric over the edge of the paper, being careful not to fold the paper itself. The smooth curves on the sides of the leaves are easy to baste.

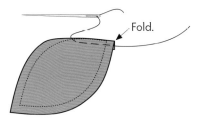

4. Baste through the freezer paper and two layers of fabric with a contrasting-color thread. Leave your thread unknotted and leave a 2" tail at the beginning. Keep your stitches in the seam allowance and smooth the fabric over the paper. There will be ripples on the wrong side—just stitch over them.

5. When you get to the point of the leaf, finger-press the extending seam allowance past the point. Fold the second side of the point back over the first side to form a clean point—this always reminds me of gift wrapping the corner of a package. Take a basting stitch into the overlapping seam allowances to hold them in place. A small tab of fabric may show on the edge; you can fold it under now or tuck it under with your needle when you appliqué.

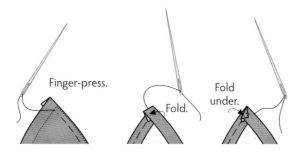

Finger-press.   Fold.   Fold under.

6. Continue basting and repeat the folding process when you get back around to the beginning point of the leaf. Leave a 2" thread tail and do not tie a knot.

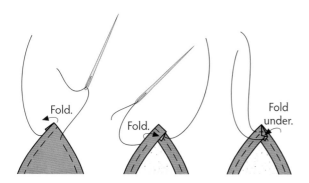

Fold.   Fold.   Fold under.

A Pointer for Outside Points

Here is another good method for preparing outside points.

1. Fold the point of the fabric in toward the appliqué. When you fold the point, don't fold it tight against the appliqué shape. Relax a little! Keep the fold 1/16" from the appliqué, and then the side folds will have room to form a sharp point.

2. Apply a small dab of glue stick to hold the folded point in place.

3. Fold the right side under, and then the left, to form a sharp point. The seam allowances may overlap slightly at the point.

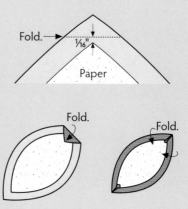

Fold.   1/16"   Paper

Fold.   Fold.

Placing and Stitching Leaves

1. Position the leaf on the background fabric, covering the placement marks and making sure the points are aligned.

2. Place four small pins, as shown, to hold the leaf in place. Pins should "point to the point" so that the pinheads are out of the way, making it easier to appliqué the points.

When a leaf is supposed to be connected to a stem, make sure the leaf touches the stem and place the pin at that point first. This will help keep it from slipping.

When a leaf is positioned under a flower, it may become a partial leaf shape. Always stitch the leaf first, and then cover the edges with the flower. In this design, stitch a complete leaf under the flower; later in your journey, as you work with other patterns, there may be situations when you appliqué just part of a leaf.

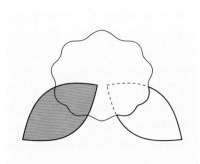

3. Because this leaf is attached to a stem, start stitching about ½" in front of the stem. This will keep the leaf in place; if you start at the outside point, the leaf may shift as you stitch around to the stem.

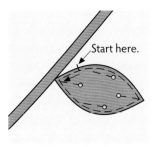

Start here.

4. Referring to "Hand-Appliqué Stitch Techniques" on page 21 for detailed instructions, slip your needle under the seam allowance on the wrong side and bring your needle out at the edge of the fold. This will hide the knot and tail of thread under the appliqué. Stitch to the point of the leaf.

5. At the first point, take one or two stitches from the leaf to the stem so that the pieces appear to be attached.

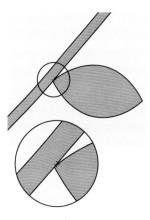

6. As you stitch the curve of the leaf, you can sweep your needle under the leaf to smooth the edge of the leaf just before you appliqué it.

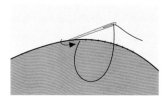

7. When you reach the outer point, sew the last stitch on the first side of the piece very close to the point. Take one extra lock stitch in the exact same place before you switch sides at the point. This extra stitch will hold your fabric securely as you turn the point and adjust the fabric on the second side.

Lock stitch

8. Before you stitch past the point, gently pull your thread in the direction of the point. This will accent the shape.

9. Place the next stitch on the opposite side of the point. A stitch on each side, close to the point, will accent the outside point. To avoid flattening the point, don't put a stitch directly on it.

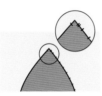

10. If a small tab of seam allowance extends beyond the edge of the appliqué, use your needle to push it under the appliqué before you stitch. Don't cut it off!

11. Stitch all the way around the leaf, adding a few stitches to overlap your beginning stitches. Bring your needle through to the back of your project, tie two little knots, hide the thread tail under the leaf, and clip the thread.

12. Referring to "Removing Basting and Paper" on page 24, remove the basting stitches and paper from the leaf.

BUDS

The buds in the Baltimore block consist of the calyx (the base of the bud) and the actual folded piece that creates the bud.

Cutting and Preparing Folded Buds

1. To make the folded bud, cut a 2½" x 2½" square of fabric.

2. Fold the square in half diagonally, wrong sides together.

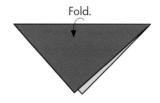

Fold.

3. Fold each side point downward to the center point, overlapping the points so that they are about ¼" from the bottom point. Baste along the bottom edges of the folded bud. You can fold all of the buds in the same manner, or you can fold them so that one has the right side on top and one has the left side on top. Fold and baste both of your buds at the same time to give them a consistent look.

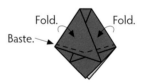

Fold.   Fold.
Baste.

Cutting and Preparing the Calyx

1. Cut the calyx on the bias. This will help the bottom curve smoothly and prevent the inside point at the top from fraying. Add a generous ¼" seam allowance around the freezer paper when you cut out the calyx fabric.

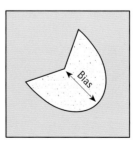

Bias

2. Baste the top edge of the calyx. Clip the inside point so that the fabric will turn over the edge. Stop clipping about ¹⁄₁₆" from the paper.

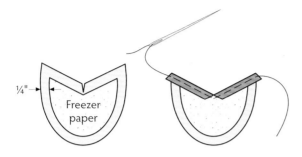

3. Fold the first point (see "Cutting and Preparing Leaves" on page 27).

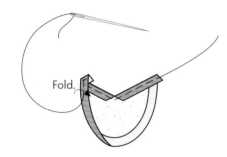

4. Baste the outside curve by moving your needle to the seam allowance on the back and making small running stitches in the seam allowance only. Don't baste through the paper and the right side of the fabric. Gently pull the thread to gather the fabric and ease the seam allowance around the curve for a smooth fit.

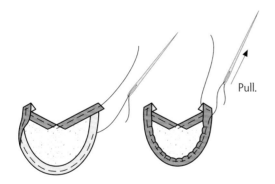

5. Continue by folding and basting the second point. Continue to baste, overlapping your basting stitches along the top edge.

Placing and Stitching the Buds

1. Place the calyx on the background fabric, covering the placement marks and the end of the stem. Insert three small pins, as shown, to hold the calyx in place. Position the pins in the corners so that they "point to the point" as for leaves, making it easy to appliqué the points.

2. Start stitching at the top edge of the calyx, about ¹⁄₈" from a point. Leave the top edge open to insert the folded bud last.

3. Appliqué the first point, and then continue around the curve and over the second point, leaving the top edge unstitched. If little points appear along the curve, use the tip of your needle to smooth them out when you sew the appliqué to the background.

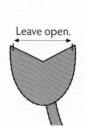

4. Use tweezers to gently insert the folded bud into the calyx, making sure that the basting stitches of the bud disappear into the calyx. (If desired, you can remove the freezer paper from the calyx before appliquéing it along the top.)

5. Appliqué the top of the calyx, making sure that the stitches will hold the bud securely in the calyx. To do this, use "stab stitches" going through all layers at each end and in the middle. The outer edges of the folded bud are not stitched to the background.

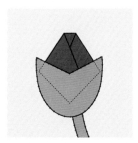

6. Remove the basting stitches from the calyx. The basting stitches on the folded piece can remain, as they are hidden inside the calyx.

7. To remove the freezer paper, make a small cut in the background behind the calyx and pull the paper out with tweezers (unless you already removed the freezer paper from the top of the calyx before inserting the folded bud).

CIRCLES AND BERRIES

The circles that create the berries for the Baltimore blocks in this book all finish at ¾" in diameter. There are many methods for cutting and preparing circles. Here I've included techniques that work best for me and that have been successful for my students.

Cutting and Preparing Circles

To draw circles, whether onto paper or fabric, I like to use a plastic stencil with circles in multiple sizes. Available at office- or art-supply stores, this handy tool makes it easy to draw perfectly shaped circles, every time.

Use heavy paper, such as a manila folder, to make templates for circles. You can also use "Perfect Circles," heat-resistant plastic circle templates; these are available at your favorite quilt shop or at www.karenkay-buckley.com. These templates can be reused, making paper templates unnecessary.

1. Trace a ¾" circle onto heavy paper, using either a plastic stencil or the circle pattern provided above right.

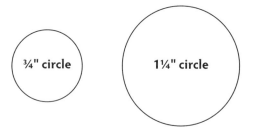

Have a Penny?

You can also trace around a penny—it's the perfect size!

¾" circle

1¼" circle

2. Cut out the paper circle, cutting as slowly and smoothly as possible. Use small, sharp scissors for best results, following up with a nail file to smooth any points or bumps along the edges. Make one paper template for each appliquéd circle.

3. Use the circle stencil again to trace a 1¼" circle onto your fabric. This adds a ¼" seam allowance around the outer edge. Cut out the fabric circle on the line. You can also trace the 1¼" circle pattern above onto freezer paper and use it to cut out your fabric circles.

4. Using a small running stitch, sew within the seam allowance around the fabric circle, leaving at least a 2" tail of thread at the beginning. Keep the stitches within the seam allowance, but not too close to the edge. When you get all the way around, tie a single knot with the two thread ends and leave the thread ends loose.

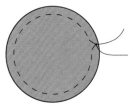

5. Working on your ironing surface, place a ¾" paper template in the center of the fabric circle, on the wrong side. Pull the thread ends to draw the seam allowance around the template. You can pin the circle to the pad of your ironing board with a big straight pin so that your hands will be free to pull

the threads and adjust the fabric around the paper template.

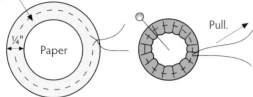

Wrong side of fabric

¼"

Paper

Pull.

6. Steam press the fabric circle, using spray starch if you like, and then let it cool for a minute.

7. Carefully peel back the fabric and remove the paper circle. Gently pull the basting threads to tighten the seam allowance again and make it lie flat. Tie another knot to secure the gathers, and trim the threads.

Placing and Stitching Circles

1. For circles, use a small dab of glue when you place your shape in the desired position on your background fabric. Pins can sometimes distort the circle. I do use pins on larger circles occasionally, but glue is always a safe choice.

2. Slip your threaded needle into the seam allowance of the circle and bring your needle out at the edge of the fold. This will hide the thread tail and keep your work neat.

3. Appliqué the circle with smaller-than-usual stitches. For impressively small stitches, sew around the circle twice. The second time, place your stitches between the stitches from the first round. You do not have to remove the basting thread; it will be hidden inside your circle.

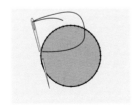

LAYERED ROSE

The layered rose is composed of the base flower, which is appliquéd first, followed by the flower center and then the two petals. The layering adds dimension and interest to the rose.

Cutting and Preparing the Rose

1. Using freezer paper, make a template for the base of the rose and two templates for the teardrop petals, tracing directly from the pattern (page 60).

2. Iron the freezer-paper templates to the wrong side of the rose fabrics and cut them out adding a ¼" seam allowance. Place the petal templates on the bias so that the curve will turn smoothly. The base of the rose can be placed on the straight of grain.

3. The base of the rose includes a series of inner and outer curves. Make double clips, stopping ¹⁄₁₆" from the paper, on the inner curves for smooth turning. (One clip will create an inner point.) Don't clip the outside curve, because clipping there will create little points along the edge of the appliqué.

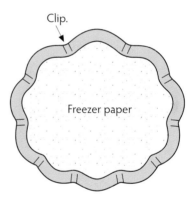

Clip.

Freezer paper

4. Carefully baste around the base of the rose, keeping the edges smooth and using small stitches to catch the clipped areas and to baste little tucks around the outer curves.

5. For the teardrop petals, start basting at the point and take about four stitches.

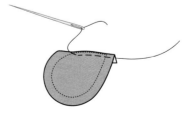

6. Move your needle to the back of the petal into the seam allowance. Baste the outside curve by making small running stitches *in the seam allowance only.* Continue basting in the seam allowance until you are four stitches from the point. Gently pull the thread to gather the fabric and ease the seam allowance around the curve for a smooth fit.

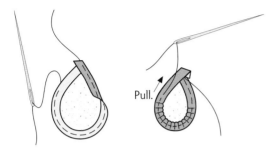

7. Baste through the paper again. Before you get to the point, finger-press the beginning seam allowance, extending it past the point.

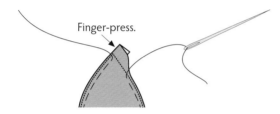

8. Fold the second side of the point back over the first side to form a clean point—just like wrapping the corner of a package. Take a basting stitch into the overlapping seam allowances to hold them in place. A small tab of fabric may show on the edge; you can fold it under now or tuck it under with your needle when you appliqué. Leave a 2" thread tail and do not tie a knot.

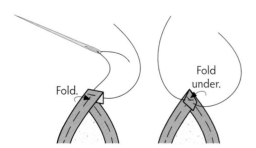

9. Cut and prepare a 1¼" circle from the fabric for the center of the rose, following the instructions for the berry circles beginning on page 32. The circle will finish at ¾".

Placing and Stitching the Rose

When you appliqué the base of the rose, the placement lines for the center and petals will be covered up by the appliqué. Make a window template for perfect placement of the rose center and petals.

1. Trace the outline and pieces of the rose pattern onto plain paper. Cut out the outer rose shape, and then carefully cut out the center and petals to create a window.

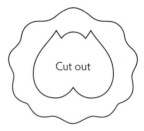

Cut out

2. Pin the base of the rose to the background fabric, making sure to center it over the markings.

3. Slip your threaded needle into the seam allowance to hide the knot, and start stitching at the center bottom to keep the rose centered between the stems. Using small stitches, carefully stitch around the base of the rose, appliquéing the inner and outer curves. On the inner curves, sweep your needle under the edge of the appliqué to smooth the edges. If little points appear along the outer curve, control them with the tip of your needle by pushing the fabric against the edge of the paper. Remove the basting stitches and freezer-paper template.

Thinking Ahead

If you plan to quilt around the petals, it helps to trim away the background fabric behind the base of the rose after you appliqué it. Leave a ¼"-wide seam allowance inside the appliqué stitches and then appliqué the petals on top.

4. Place the paper window over the appliquéd flower piece. Position the center circle, using a dab of glue to hold it in position, and appliqué it to the base.

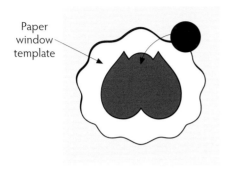

5. Place the paper window template over the appliquéd flower piece and use it to position one petal. Pin as shown, placing one pin near the point so that it "points to the point."

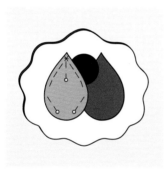

6. Appliqué the petal and remove the basting stitches and freezer paper.

7. Using the window template, layer the second petal over the center circle and the first petal, and stitch the second petal in place. Due to the multiple layers of fabric, your stitches may go through all the layers or only through some of them. Either way, the petal will be securely attached.

8. Remove the basting and freezer paper from the second petal.

BIRD

The bird is the last element of the design to be appliquéd. You will appliqué the bird's body first, and then place the wing on top. You're almost done!

Cutting and Preparing the Bird

1. Make one freezer-paper template for the bird and one for the wing. The bird template must be cut in reverse because the bird is asymmetrical. Make a plastic template (page 17), flip the template over, and trace it onto freezer paper. The wing is symmetrical, so you can trace it directly from the pattern.

2. Iron the freezer-paper templates to the wrong side of your bird fabrics. The bird body can be positioned in any direction, but the wing should be placed and cut on the bias.

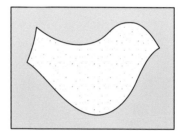 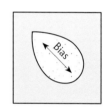

3. Cut out the bird and the wing, adding a generous ¼" seam allowance around the freezer paper.

4. The bird has some areas that are inner curves; clip these halfway through the seam allowance so that they will turn easily over the freezer paper. Make several clips about ⅛" apart in the curve. This will help create a smooth curve as you baste and appliqué.

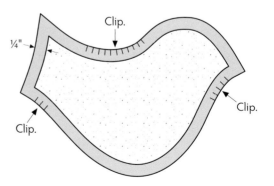

5. Fold the outer points of the tail and the beak in the same manner as the points on the leaves (see "Cutting and Preparing Leaves" on page 27).

6. Baste the bird's wing, following the directions for the teardrop petals of the rose (see "Cutting and Preparing the Rose" on page 33).

Placing and Stitching the Bird

1. Pin the bird to the background fabric, aligning the shape with the placement lines.

2. Slip your threaded needle into the seam allowance, hiding the knot. Start stitching on the bird's back, leaving open the area that will be under the wing.

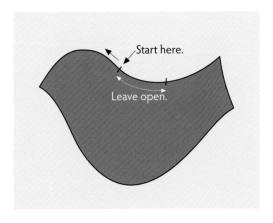

3. As you stitch the inner and outer curves, sweep your needle under the edge of the appliqué to smooth the edges.

4. At the points, make a stitch on each side, close to the point, to accent the outside point. Don't put a stitch directly on the point because it might flatten the point. (See "Placing and Stitching Leaves" on page 28.)

5. When you have stitched around the bird and are back along the top where the wing goes, remove the basting stitches and the freezer paper with tweezers before you add the wing.

6. Pin the wing on the bird as shown and appliqué it in place. Where the wing overlaps the bird, you can choose to have your stitches go all the way through to the back, or simply through the bird. Remove the freezer paper from the wing before completing the stitching, if desired.

7. Clip and remove the basting stitches. Remove the freezer paper under the wing, if you haven't already done so, by making a small clip in the background on the wrong side, just under the point of the wing.

8. For the bird's eye, attach a bead or embroider a French knot as shown.

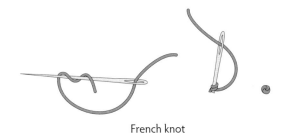

French knot

Assembling Your First Baltimore Quilt

After you have finished your appliqué block, follow these basic steps to assemble your quilt top with setting triangles and borders.

WASHING YOUR BLOCK

When you finish stitching, always wash your appliquéd quilt block. This removes any pencil marks, glue-stick residue, or finger smudges as needed.

1. Simply run warm water in the sink with some mild soap. Place the block in the water and soak it for a while, then rinse it with water until there are no more soap bubbles. Try not to wrinkle it or wring it dry.

2. Place the block, right side down, on a clean towel. Roll it up to get out most of the moisture, then unroll it and let it dry flat.

3. If you've used glue to prepare your appliqués, cut a slit in the background fabric behind each piece and gently remove the freezer-paper templates.

4. Lay the block right side down on top of a towel and press with a steam iron to enhance the dimensional appliqué. Then press the edges on the ironing-board surface. Now it's clean and neat and ready to be squared up before you sew it into your quilt.

TRIMMING AND SQUARING UP YOUR BLOCK

Before you stitch your block into the quilt, trim it to size and square it up, keeping the design centered.

If your piece of background fabric is a perfect 15" square, you can trim the block to 13½" by carefully trimming ¾" off of each side. Simply measure ¾" with a ruler, draw a line, and then cut on the line with scissors or a rotary cutter.

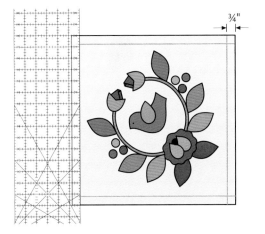

If your background piece is not a perfect 15" square after appliquéing, cut a 13½" square from transparent template plastic. Mark diagonal lines on the square with a pencil, and then place the plastic over your appliquéd block, using the lines to center the design. Draw around the edges and then cut on the drawn lines with scissors or a rotary cutter.

ADDING SETTING TRIANGLES

You will sew setting triangles cut from your inspiration fabric to the sides of your block to frame it and make it a square before adding borders.

1. Mark the center of each triangle by folding the long edge of the triangle in half and marking the center with a pin. Then mark the center of the block edge by folding it in half and marking the center with a pin.

2. Center a setting triangle on one side of your block, matching the centers. Pin the triangle to the block, right sides together. Add a second triangle to the opposite side of the block. The triangles will extend slightly (⅜") past the edges of the block equally at both ends.

3. Sew the triangles to the block with ¼" seam allowances. Press the seam allowances toward the triangles.

4. Repeat with the other two triangles on the remaining sides. Press the seam allowances toward the triangles.

ADDING BORDERS

Take your time measuring, cutting, and sewing your borders so that they will be smooth and flat. It's always a good idea to measure your quilt before cutting and attaching borders. Even on a small quilt, your assembled quilt top may vary in size from the pattern measurements. Measure your quilt through the center in both directions. Center measurements are most accurate because the edges of the quilt may have stretched during assembly.

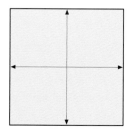

Measure center of quilt.

The inner borders accent the inspiration fabric. I like to use inner borders that finish from 1" to 1¼" wide because these narrow strips do not require quilting. You can simply quilt on either side of the inner borders. The outer borders are cut from your inspiration fabric and will frame your quilt.

1. Measure the vertical center of the quilt and cut two side-border strips to this measurement. Fold the quilt in half and mark the center of each side with a pin. Fold each border strip in half crosswise and mark the center with a pin. Match the centers of the border and the quilt; pin together. Continue to

pin together, easing the edge of the quilt to fit the border if necessary.

2. Sew a side-border strip to the quilt. Press seam allowances toward the border. Repeat for the other side.

3. Using the same process, measure the quilt horizontally (including the two side borders), cut the strips, and then sew the top and bottom inner-border strips to the quilt, overlapping the two side borders. Press the seam allowances toward the border.

4. Repeat step 1 to cut the strips, and then sew the outer-border strips to the sides of your quilt. Press the seam allowances toward the inner border. This will make it easy to quilt on either side of the inner border.

5. Repeat the measuring, cutting, and sewing process for the top and bottom outer-border strips. Press the seam allowances toward the inner border.

Finishing Your First Baltimore Quilt

Congratulations! You're ready to finish your first Baltimore appliqué quilt by quilting it and adding a hanging sleeve, binding, and a special label. If you need help with these details, you can refer to instructions on the Martingale website, or use it as an excuse to take a class at your favorite quilt shop!

After assembling your quilt top, layer it with batting and backing and quilt your masterpiece. Your quilting stitches will outline and define the appliqué pieces. Quilting stitches also create a design in the background area that adds a wonderful texture to your quilt. There's not enough space in this book to cover quilting details, but many excellent books and classes are available on the subject. Before you quilt by hand or machine, refer to "Quilting Sequence" at right for some helpful hints.

MAKING A LABEL

You've created a very special quilt and now you need to sign it! Here are some suggestions for making a label and adding your signature.

Make a label for the back of your quilt that includes the name of the quilt, your name, and the date. Include information about the quilt, a dedication, or a personal story about your quilt.

Design your own label or trace a design from a book or other source. Add lettering with embroidery stitches or a permanent marking pen and attach the label to your quilt with the traditional appliqué stitch.

My First Baltimore Block
stitched by
Mimi Dietrich
2012

Quilting Sequence

Whether you make a quilt with one block or a full-sized quilt, I recommend this sequence for quilting an appliquéd quilt.

1. Quilt around the outside edges of all appliqué pieces in the quilt block. Place stitches just outside the appliqué edge, stitching through the quilt background, batting, and backing. This outline quilting will accent your designs and make your appliqué pieces puff slightly. This technique is sometimes called *quilting in the ditch.*

2. Quilt along the inner edges of the setting triangles where they adjoin the quilt block. Quilt the inner and outer edges of the narrow inner border of your quilt. Be careful to keep these lines straight so that the quilt doesn't become distorted.

3. Quilt the background design in the center of the quilt.

4. Quilt the background design in the setting triangles and borders if desired.

HAPPY DANCE

Wow, you've finished your quilt! Turn on your favorite music, call your best friend, break out the champagne, and do a happy dance. Celebrate!

I hope these step-by-step basics have helped you make your first Baltimore appliqué quilt. I also hope that you are inspired to make a second appliqué quilt, take appliqué classes, stitch more designs from appliqué patterns and books . . . and eventually make a full-sized appliqué quilt!

Special Techniques

Once you've learned basic appliqué techniques, it's fun to incorporate special touches with dimensional appliqué; embroidery; embellishments such as beads, buttons, and trims; or motifs cut from fabric. Add seed beads, other small beads, or embroidery stitches in the centers of the flowers.

GATHERED BLOSSOMS

Gathered blossoms create a ring of lovely violets surrounding the appliquéd bird.

Gathered blossoms enhance your block with lovely small flowers that add texture and dimension. You can substitute gathered blossoms for the berries or the folded buds.

Choose lightweight cotton fabric in a color to coordinate with other flowers or fabrics in your quilt. Heavier fabrics may not gather easily. If possible, use heavy quilting thread or all-purpose thread that matches your fabric to gather your flower. Lightweight thread may break.

Cutting and Preparing Gathered Blossoms

1. Trace the 3"-diameter circle pattern on page 42 onto freezer paper. Cut out the circle.

2. Iron the freezer-paper circle onto your fabric (either the right or wrong side) and cut around the edges to make a 3" fabric circle. Gently remove the freezer paper.

3. Use a doubled length of thread about 18" long and tie a knot in the end. Hold the circle so that you are looking at the wrong side of the fabric. Turn under ⅛" around the edge of the circle and sew a running stitch near the fold.

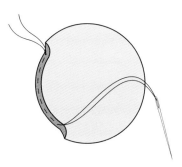

4. Gather the edges in the center of the circle (like a yo-yo) and tie a secure knot. If the edges don't meet tightly, take a few back-and-forth stitches at the center, like a spiderweb pattern, to close the hole.

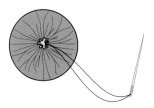

5. Insert the needle straight down through the center of the gathers, bringing it through to the back (flat) side.

6. With the gathered side up, divide the circle into five equal petals as shown, marking lightly with a fabric marker or small pins.

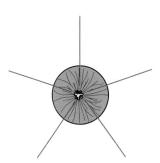

7. To make the petals, bring the needle and thread from the back over the outside edge of the flower (on the marked line) and insert the needle into the center again. Hint: to hide the threads, insert the needle between folds approximately ⅛" out from the center. Position the thread at one of the edge markings, and then pull the thread to create a petal.

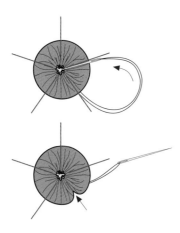

8. Continue looping the thread over the edges to make five petals. Knot the thread on the back of the blossom. Tie a second knot and then cut the thread off near the needle, leaving the threads to be used later for attaching the blossom to the quilt.

9. Stitch three seed beads to the flower center, one at a time, using thread that matches the beads.

Placing and Stitching Gathered Blossoms

Wait until you have quilted your quilt to add the gathered blossoms. Otherwise, the quilting thread might tangle around the blossoms as you take your quilting stitches.

After you have quilted, thread a needle with the double thread from the blossom. Tack the blossom to the background fabric by stitching two or three times through the background and the center of the blossom. Take the thread to the back of the quilt, tie a knot, slip the thread under the backing, and cut the thread.

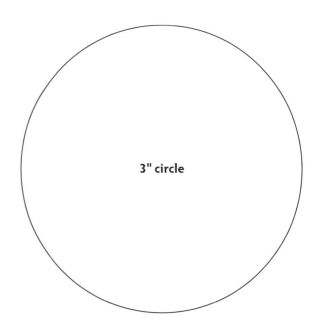

3" circle

GATHERED FLOWERS

A gathered flower can be a dramatic focal point for your Baltimore block.

Gathered flowers are made with a technique known as *ruching*. You can substitute these lovely textured flowers for the layered rose in the Baltimore block, or for a larger flower in any appliqué design.

Use lightweight cotton for these flowers—you will need fabric that gathers easily. Choose a tone-on-tone print or a fabric with splashes of color. Avoid small-scale prints, because the design will simply get lost in the gathers. Just as with gathered blossoms, use heavy quilting thread or all-purpose thread that matches your fabric to gather your flower. Lightweight thread may break.

Cutting and Preparing Gathered Flowers

1. Using a rotary cutter and ruler, cut a straight-grain strip of fabric 1¼" wide and 40" long. With wrong sides together, fold the long edges of the strip toward the center so that the raw edges meet. Press.

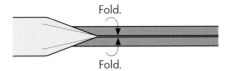

Fold.

Fold.

Easy Pressing

To fold and press the strip easily, insert a long needle into your ironing-board cover, taking two stitches and leaving ⅝" (or whatever finished width you desire) between the stitches. Leave the needle in place, fold the strip of fabric as described above, and thread it through the space. As you pull the strip under the needle, iron the folds to make a smooth strip. Use a steam iron and add spray starch to help the strip hold its shape nicely.

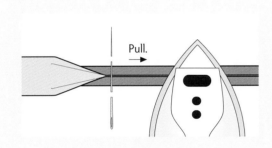

Pull.

2. Lay the folded strip right side up along the ruching guide below. Use a fabric marker to place dots along both folded edges of your strip at 1" intervals. Mark the entire strip.

3. Knot a single length of thread, about 25" long. Starting ½" from one end, sew a running stitch from dot to dot in a zigzag pattern. As you change directions, stitch over the folded edges.

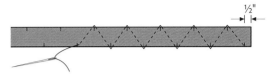

½"

4. Stitch about 6" before pulling the thread to gather the fabric. Pull the thread in a straight line, working with one diagonally stitched line at a time to gather fabric petals on each side. You need to have a few petals made or the fabric won't stay gathered.

5. Continue stitching and gently pull the gathering thread each time you change directions to prevent the thread from breaking.

6. When you are about 3" from the end and most of the strip is gathered, stop stitching. Do not tie a knot at the end. Leave the thread and needle so you can make adjustments at the end.

Gathers for Goldilocks

Gathers that are too tight will have pointed petals. Gathers that are too loose will have threads showing. Gathers that are "just right" will have rounded petals.

7. To form the flower, thread a second needle with a single 18" length of matching thread. Trim the beginning edge of the strip to ¼" and turn this seam allowance under the first petal. Tack it securely. Arrange the first five petals into a circle, and then take a stitch in each of these petals to

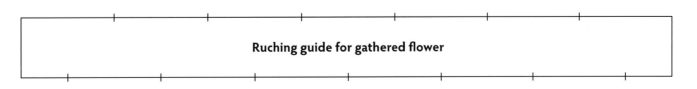

Ruching guide for gathered flower

draw them together. Take a stitch back into the first petal to form the center of your flower. Pull your thread to the back of your flower and tie a knot.

8. Carefully arrange the sixth and seventh petals slightly under the first one to begin making the second round of petals. Pin in place. Turn the flower over and tack the inside of the petals to the back as you form the flower. Keep placing the petals, pinning, and tacking. Work twice around the center of the flower.

9. When you get to the end of the flower, taper the last petal under the previous round, adjusting it to form a smooth shape. You may need to add or remove a few petals. As you finish, your gathering stitches should stop on the outside edge of the strip. Pull the thread to make the last petal, and knot the thread. Cut the strip ½" beyond the last stitch, and tuck the raw edges under the flower. Try to make the gathered strip go twice around the flower center. If the last petal is across from or opposite the first petal, the flower will be balanced.

Tuck under.

Making a Two-Color Gathered Flower

Once your flower is finished, you can add another color around the edges by gathering a lighter or darker strip and tacking it so that it encircles the flower. Simply tuck the beginning and ending tabs behind the original flower.

Placing and Stitching Gathered Flowers

After the flower is formed, start at the outside edge and appliqué the petals securely to the background fabric before quilting. Stitch the "tips" and "dips" of each petal. Your stitches will move in a spiral toward the center of the flower. When you get to the last petal at the flower center, stitch down the side of the petal to help it blend into the flower.

If you wish, stitch beads to the center of the flower, tacking the center to the background.

FABULOUS FABRICS

Your inspiration fabric may provide a perfect substitute for the bird in the center of your block.

When your fabric is printed with wonderful designs, such as flowers, birds, or butterflies, you can simply cut out the motif and use it as is in your appliqué quilt! The name for this appliqué technique is *broderie perse*. The butterfly in the quilt shown was printed on the inspiration fabric.

1. Cut out the image you wish to use, adding a scant ¼" seam allowance all the way around.

2. Use a glue stick to position the image on your background fabric so that it will lie flat and stay secure. Keep the glue at least ½" from the edge of your image.

3. Use your needle to turn the seam allowance under and stitch the image to your background. Clip inner points and curves to allow easy turning of the seam allowance. This technique is called "needle-turn" appliqué.

4. Embroider any embellishments that seem appropriate, such as the antennae on the featured butterfly, using one strand of embroidery thread and the chain stitch or stem stitch as shown.

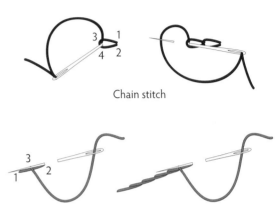

Chain stitch

Stem stitch or outline stitch

A Gallery of First Baltimore Quilts

Romantic Roses.
Appliquéd by Mimi Dietrich, hand quilted by Norma Campbell.

Tradition!
Appliquéd and hand quilted by Libbie Rollman.

A Gallery of First Baltimore Quilts

Mod Dots.
Appliquéd by Mimi Dietrich, machine quilted by Maria O'Haver.

Autumn Batik.
Appliquéd by Mimi Dietrich, machine quilted by Maria O'Haver.

Mimi substituted berries for the buds at the top of the stems.

Free Bird.
Appliquéd by Mimi Dietrich, machine quilted by Karen Brown.

Mimi substituted gathered blossoms and flowers for the berries and layered rose.

Wild Thing!
Appliquéd by Mimi Dietrich, hand quilted by Norma Campbell.

A butterfly cut from the inspiration fabric replaces the bird in the center of the wreath.

Oriental Delight.
Appliquéd by Mimi Dietrich, machine quilted by Maria O'Haver.

Gathered blossoms and flowers add dimension to the "Crossed Leaves" pattern.

Black & White & A Little Red Bird.
Appliquéd by Mimi Dietrich, machine quilted by Karen Brown.

The red bird, berries, and inner border accent the dramatic black-and-white prints in this quilt made using the "Round Wreath" pattern.

Gathered Sweet Violets.
Appliquéd by Mimi Dietrich, machine quilted by Maria O'Haver.

Gathered blossoms add dimension to the "Round Wreath" pattern.

Bluebird of Happiness.
Appliquéd by Emily Pelton, machine quilted by Maria O'Haver.

Emily substituted a gathered flower for the layered rose on her first appliquéd block.

Baltimore Block Patterns

MY FIRST BALTIMORE BLOCK

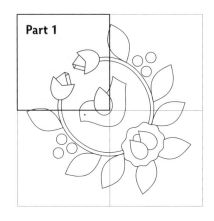
Part 1

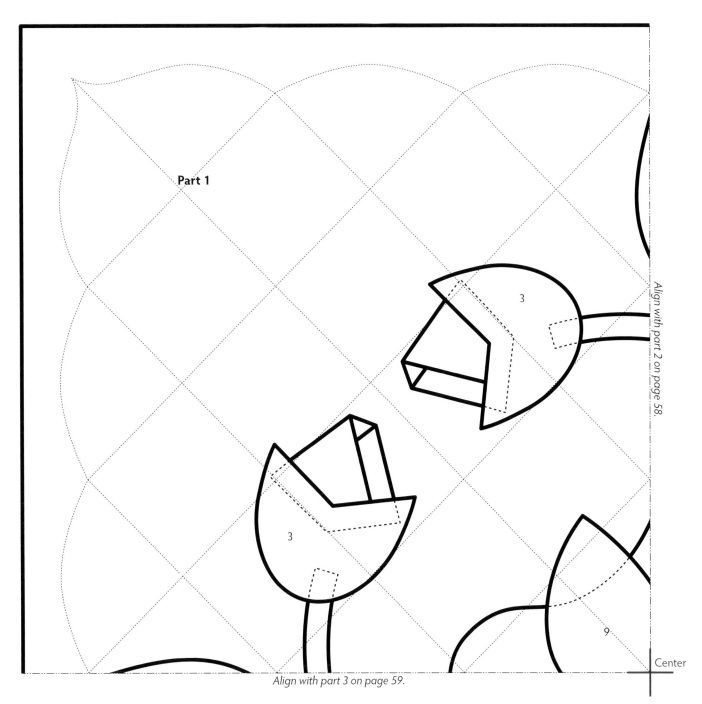

Part 1

3

3

9

Align with part 2 on page 58.

Center

Align with part 3 on page 59.

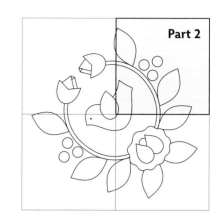

Part 2

Align with part 1 on page 57.

Center

Align with part 4 on page 60.

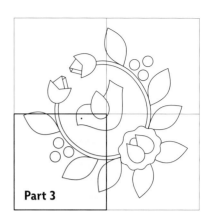

Part 3

Align with part 1 on page 57.

Center

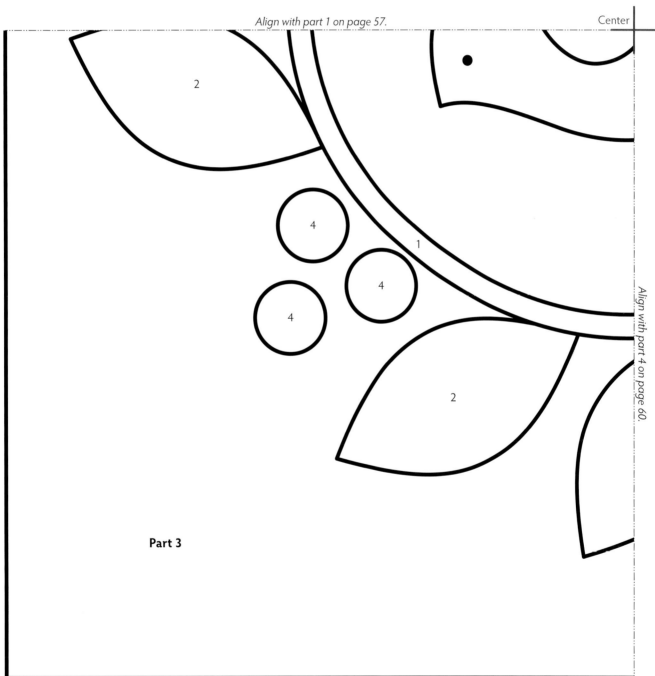

2

4

1

4

4

2

Align with part 4 on page 60

Part 3

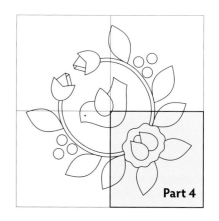

Part 4

Center

Align with part 2 on page 58.

Align with part 3 on page 59.

8

2

5

6

7

7

2

2

2

Part 4

ROUND WREATH

Use the chain stitch on page 45 to embroider the berry stems.

2

3

2

3

1

Add the bird (4) and wing (5) from "My First Baltimore Block" (pieces 8 and 9 on pages 57–60) to the center of the block.

4

5

Center

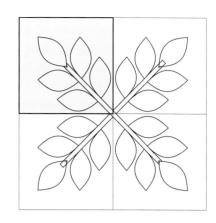

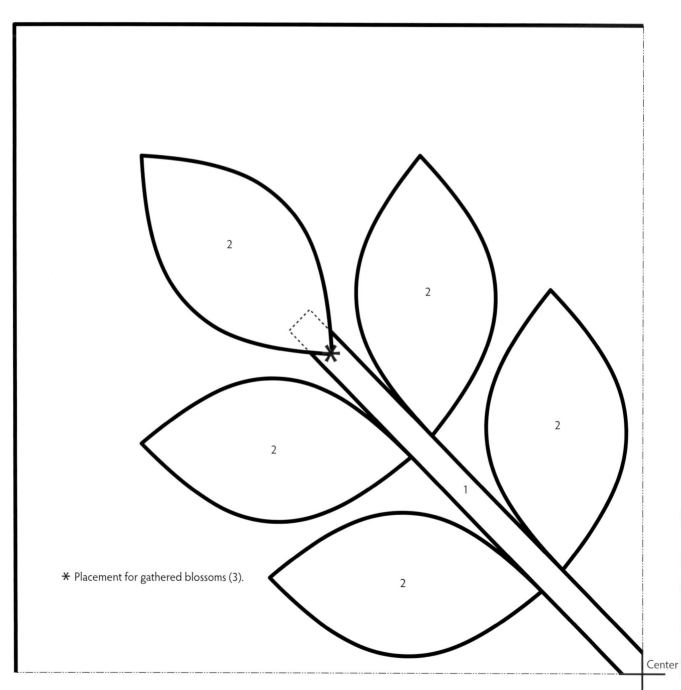

✱ Placement for gathered blossoms (3).

2

2

2

2

2

1

Center

Appliqué Glossary

Here are definitions of some common appliqué terms that you may find helpful.

Appliqué: A method of sewing pieces of fabric on top of a larger background-fabric piece to create a design.

Appliqué stitch: A small, nearly invisible stitch used to attach appliqué fabric to the background fabric.

Background fabric: A large piece of fabric to which appliqué shapes are stitched.

Basting: Temporarily holding fabric in place by stitching, pinning, or gluing.

Bias: A diagonal line that runs at a 45° angle to the threads in the fabric. Fabric has the greatest amount of stretch on the bias.

Broderie perse: Cutting a design for appliqué from a printed fabric.

Freezer-paper appliqué: A method of preparing appliqué shapes using templates cut from freezer paper.

Fussy cutting: Cutting an appliqué piece from a specific area of a fabric design, such as leaves or flowers.

Glue basting: Using a dab of glue stick to temporarily hold fabric in place.

Hand appliqué: Stitching the appliqués to the background fabric using hand-sewing techniques.

Hand basting: Using a hand-sewing needle, thread, and running stitches to temporarily hold fabric in place.

Layered appliqué: A design with appliqués that overlap other appliquéd pieces.

Needle-turn appliqué: A method of turning the seam allowance of the appliqué pieces under as you sew them to the background fabric.

Pin basting: Using pins to temporarily hold fabric in place.

Ruching: A technique for gathering a strip of fabric to create a dimensional flower.

Seam allowance: The extra fabric outside the finished appliqué shape. The standard appliqué seam allowance is ¼" on all sides of an appliqué piece. Sometimes the directions may call for a skimpy or generous ¼" seam allowance. This means to make your seam allowance just a little narrower or wider than ¼".

Straight of grain: The straight threads that run the length (lengthwise grain) and width (crosswise grain) of the fabric.

Template: An appliqué shape cut from plastic or freezer paper, used as a pattern for tracing a design onto fabric or paper. Cut appliqué templates the finished size of the shape and don't include seam allowances.

Window template: A shape cut into a piece of paper that lets you preview fabric choices or correctly position layered appliqué pieces.

About the Author

Photo courtesy of Cara Walen photography.

Mimi Dietrich has been appliquéing for as long as she can remember! Her first quilt, made for her son Jon in 1974, featured Sunbonnet Sue and Overall Bill with a dimensional hankie in Bill's pocket. One of her most recent creations was an appliquéd quilt for Jon's daughter, Julia.

Mimi has lived in Baltimore all her life and is inspired by the beautiful Baltimore Album appliqué quilts made in her hometown more than 150 years ago. She is a "Founding Mother" of the Village Quilters and the Baltimore Appliqué Society. She teaches a yearlong appliqué class in Baltimore and encourages students to create their own special album quilts. She hopes to inspire you to start an appliquéd quilt—or finish one that's been on the back burner for too long!—with the patterns, tips, and techniques in this book.

This is Mimi's 16th book published by Martingale. Visit her online at www.mimidietrich.com.